I0448510

Informing the legislative debate since 1914 _____

Child Labor in America: History, Policy, and Legislative Issues

Gerald Mayer
Analyst in Labor Policy

November 18, 2013

Congressional Research Service

7-5700

www.crs.gov

RL31501

Summary

The history of child labor in America is long and, in some cases, unsavory. It dates back to the founding of the United States. Historically, except for the privileged few, most children worked—either for their parents or for an outside employer. Through the years, however, child labor practices have changed. So have the benefits and risks associated with employment of children. In some respects, altered workplace technology has served to make work easier and less hazardous. At the same time, some processes and equipment have rendered the workplace more advanced and dangerous, especially for children and youth.

Child labor first became a federal legislative issue at least as far back as 1906 with the introduction of the Beveridge proposal for regulation of the types of work in which children might be engaged. Although the 1906 legislation was not adopted, it led to extended study of the conditions under which children were employed or allowed to work and to a series of legislative proposals—some approved, others defeated or overturned by the courts—culminating in the Fair Labor Standards Act (FLSA) of 1938. The latter statute, amended periodically, remains the primary federal law dealing with the employment of children.

Generally speaking, work by young persons (under 18 years of age) in mines and factories is not allowed. The types of nonfarm work that may be suitable (or especially hazardous) for persons under 18 years of age has been left mainly to the discretion of the Secretary of Labor. Some types of work—for example, some newspaper sales and delivery, theatrical (and related) employment—are exempt from the FLSA child labor requirements. Finally, a distinction has been made between employment in nonagricultural occupations and in agricultural occupations and, in the latter case, between work for a parent and commercial employment.

This report examines the historical issue of child labor in America and summarizes legislation that has been introduced from the 108th Congress to the 113th Congress.

Contents

Tables

Contacts

Efforts to set standards for child labor in America largely began late in the 19th century, mostly at the state level. During the first decade of the 20th century, child labor became a federal concern. Congressional hearings were followed by extensive study of the issue—and by several unsuccessful efforts to deal with child labor through law. Finally, with the adoption of the Fair Labor Standards Act (FLSA) of 1938, the modern federal role in child labor regulation took shape.[1]

The history of child labor in the American workplace can be divided, roughly, into four periods. First, from the late 19th century to 1941, reformers sought to remove children from the workplace (whether factory, field, or tenement house) and to encourage more extended school attendance. Second, with World War II, the focus shifted to alleged labor shortages for war production. Some urged modification of work restrictions for older children: too young for the draft but old enough to be useful employees. Third, by the late 1940s, another shift took place. Too many older youths were believed to be out of school, out of work, and unable to find employment for which, it was argued, they were often unprepared both in terms of training and discipline. Thus, various "school-to-work" transition programs were developed together with "incentives" for employers to hire youth workers. Fourth, since roughly the late 1980s, child labor in its various aspects has largely disappeared from the policy scene; the issue is often viewed as a remnant of an earlier period in American history.

Debate over the regulation of child labor is often contentious, sparking sharp differences of opinion. Some have urged modification of existing federal child labor law to afford greater opportunities for young persons to learn the value of work or to gain entry into a skilled occupation. Others have questioned whether minors should be employed at all, especially while attending school. Child labor can also provide an occasion for youth to be exploited and, possibly, endangered.

This report briefly describes the early history of child labor regulation, reviews recent federal initiatives in that area, and summarizes legislation from the 108th Congress through the 113th Congress.

Early Child Labor in America

Prior to the 20th century, employment of children largely reflected socioeconomic class stratification. Where children were of working-class families, it was largely assumed that they would work—even when they were very young. Some were employed in the street trades, delivering newspapers and telegrams, shining boots and shoes, running errands, and at whatever hours the duties demanded. Others were engaged in industrial homework, in tasks often reserved for the very young who could work, usually alongside a parent or another adult, in a tenement flat in segments of garment production or in other types of work that could be performed, sometimes on a piece rate basis, in one's place of residence. Still others worked in mines or factories, most notoriously, perhaps, the "breaker boys" (who separated coal from slate and rock) in the coal mines, the child workers in the textile mills, and the helpers in the glass factories.

Agricultural labor by children seems always to have been in a category by itself. Usually, until the early 20th century, such work seems to have been on the family farm (whatever its size) or in an

---

[1] Regulations that implement the child labor provisions of the Fair Labor Standards Act are at 29 C.F.R. Part 570.

agricultural operation in the general vicinity of a youth's place of residence, though he (or she) might reside and work beyond the view and reach of a parent.

Regulation of child labor has been motivated by diverse concerns: economic, humane, and more broadly social. In the 19th and early 20th centuries, child workers were often viewed as an alternative source of low-wage labor who vied with their parents and other adults for employment—even at the cost of their own health and education. Products of child labor competed with goods produced by adults, exerting a downward pressure on wages and living standards. Aside from health and safety hazards, inadequate rest, it was argued, left children ill-suited for educational activities and, in turn, as adults, ill-prepared for employment or for the support of their own children, thus extending the cycle of poverty and adding to social-welfare costs.[2]

Opposition to Child Labor Begins to Organize

Early on, the trade union movement voiced strong opposition to child labor. New York labor activist Samuel Gompers championed child labor reform during the late 19th century and later, as president of the American Federation of Labor (AFL), used his influence to improve the lot of working children.[3] Workers advocate "Mother" (Mary Harris) Jones brought added visibility to the plight of child workers and to that of their parents as well.[4] After its organization in 1899, the National Consumers League (NCL), under the leadership of Florence Kelley, took up the campaign against child labor, as did a significant body of social workers, clergy, and concerned individuals.[5] In 1904, these forces were drawn together with the establishment of the National Child Labor Committee (NCLC) which, thereafter, would remain a central force in the movement to end the exploitation of children in the workplace.[6]

---

[2] An extensive literature exists on child labor in America during the late 19th and early 20th centuries. See, for example Edward N. Clopper, *Child Labor in the City Streets* (New York: The Macmillan Company, 1912); Katharine DuPre Lumpkin, and Dorothy Wolff Douglas, *Child Workers in America* (New York: Robert M. McBride & Company, 1937); Edwin Markham, Benjamin B. Lindsey, and George Creel, *Children In Bondage* (New York: Hearst's International Library Co., 1914); John Spargo, *The Bitter Cry of the Children* (New York: The Macmillan Company, 1906); and John William Larner, Jr., "The Glass House Boys: Child Labor Conditions in Pittsburgh's Glass Factories, 1890-1917," *The Western Pennsylvania Historical Magazine*, October 1965, pp. 355-364.

[3] Robert H. Bremner, *From the Depths: The Discovery of Poverty in the United States* (New York: New York University Press, 1964). Page 218 notes: "The labor unions had been active in the [child labor] movement since the days of the Knights of Labor in the 1880's, and Gompers only slightly exaggerated the facts when he declared [in 1906]: 'There is not a child labor law on the statute books of the United States but has been put there by the efforts of the trade-union movement.'" But, he added: "It is unlikely ... that the campaign against child labor would have made such rapid headway after 1900 had it not been for the pressure brought to bear on both public opinion and legislatures by voluntary groups such as the consumers' leagues, state charities aid associations, federations of women's clubs, and the child-labor committees." See also Samuel Gompers, *Labor and the Common Welfare* (New York: E. P. Dutton & Company, 1919), p. 129; Jeremy P. Felt, *Hostages of Fortune: Child Labor Reform in New York State* (Syracuse: Syracuse University Press, 1965), pp. 10-13, 60, and 196-197; and Roger W. Walker, "The A.F.L. and Child-Labor Legislation: An Exercise in Frustration," *Labor History*, summer 1970, pp. 323-340.

[4] Mary Field Parton (ed.), *The Autobiography of Mother Jones* (Chicago: Charles H. Kerr Publishing Company, 1980), pp. 71-83, 118-131.

[5] Concerning the work of the National Consumers' League, see Josephine Goldmark, *Impatient Crusader* (Urbana: University of Illinois Press, 1953), a biography of Florence Kelley; Kathryn K. Sklar, *Florence Kelley and the Nation's Work*, (New Haven: Yale University Press, 1995); and Landon R. Y. Storrs, *Civilizing Capitalism: The National Consumers' League, Women's Activism, and Labor Standards in the New Deal Era* (Chapel Hill: University of North Carolina Press, 2000). (Hereafter cited as Storrs, *Civilizing Capitalism*.)

[6] Walter I. Trattner, *Crusade for the Children: A History of the National Child Labor Committee and Child Labor* (continued...)

The regulation of child labor generally began at the state level. Initial laws were often loosely drawn and, where they exerted a restraining influence, subject to court challenge. Each type of work by children—for example, in the mines, factories, fields, or street trades—presented its own special challenges for reformers. Industrial homework by children was especially difficult to restrain. Although often not formally employed, children worked in tenement sweatshops making clothing, processing food, and engaging in whatever other work might profitably be conducted at home. Any tenement might become a little factory where conditions were often adverse and hours of work were unrestrained. Thus, child labor and industrial homework, from a regulatory/reform perspective, became intermeshed. Reformers tended to agree that child labor could not be controlled while industrial homework continued.[7]

Reformers, however, did not always agree on timing or overall strategy. Most seem to have concurred that, ultimately, reform would need to be federal. Faced with state regulation of child labor or industrial homework, employers could simply move to another state. Further, those who utilized child labor could play one jurisdiction against another. At the same time, the strength of reform organization varied from one state to another. Some believed that state action was more nearly feasible than securing broader national change, at least at that time.

The Early Federal Role in Child Labor Regulation

In 1906, Senator Albert Beveridge (R-IN) and Representative Herbert Parsons (R-NY) introduced legislation to prevent the employment of children in factories and mines. Debate on this first federal initiative continued for several years but it did not become law. However, with the work of the various reform groups, the proposal raised the visibility of child labor as a public policy issue.[8] In 1907, legislation was approved (P.L. 59-41) that authorized the Secretary of Commerce and Labor (then, a single department) "to investigate and report upon the industrial, social, moral, education[al], and physical condition of woman and child workers in the United States." The result was a detailed survey which appeared in 19 volumes between 1910 and 1913.[9] Building from that evidentiary record, Congress turned again to the legislative process to deal with child labor and related problems.

(...continued)

Reform in America (Chicago: Quadrangle Books, 1970). (Hereafter cited as Trattner, *Crusade for the Children.*) For a discussion of the politics of child labor reform during this early period, see Hugh C. Bailey, *Edgar Gardner Murphy: Gentle Progressive* (Coral Gables: University of Miami Press, 1968), pp. 65-108; and Herbert J. Doherty, Jr., "Alexander J. McKelway: Preacher to Progressive," *Journal of Southern History*, May 1958, pp. 177-190.

[7] Ruth E. Shallcross, *Industrial Homework: An Analysis of Homework Regulations, Here and Abroad* (New York: Industrial Affairs Publishing Co., 1939); Eileen Boris, *Home to Work: Motherhood and the Politics of Industrial Homework in the United States* (New York: Cambridge University Press, 1994); and Ruth Crawford, "Development and Control of Industrial Homework," *Monthly Labor Review*, June 1944, pp. 1145-1158.

[8] John Braeman, "Albert J. Beveridge and the First National Child Labor Bill," *Indiana Magazine of History*, March 1964, pp. 1-36.

[9] U.S. Congress, Senate, 61st Cong., 2nd sess., Document No. 645. *Report on Condition of Woman and Child Wage-Earners in the United States*, 19 Volumes, Washington, U.S. GPO, 1913. See also U.S. Department of Labor, Bureau of Labor Statistics, Women in Industry Series No. 5, *Summary of the Report on Condition of Woman and Child Wage Earners in the United States*, Washington, GPO, 1916, 445 p.

The Child Labor Initiatives (1916-1924)

Although Congress and the advocates of reform sought to limit oppressive child labor, the best approach was not immediately clear. Thus, sequentially, Congress moved in three directions—each uniformly unsuccessful.

In 1916, a decade after the Beveridge proposal, new federal child labor legislation was introduced by Senator Robert Owen (D-OK) and by Representative Edward Keating (D-CO) with support from the reform community. A regional struggle then in progress pitted one state against another in a contest for economic growth with low-wage nonunion labor a bargaining chip. Southern manufacturers viewed child labor restrictions as an "effort of northern agitators to kill the infant industries of the south."[10] The Owen-Keating Act (1916), based on the commerce clause of the U.S. Constitution, sought to ban the movement in interstate commerce of certain products of child labor. In June 1918, however, the U.S. Supreme Court declared the act unconstitutional (*Hammer v. Dagenhart*, 247 U.S. 251), and reformers searched for a new approach.[11]

Congress next turned to its taxing power as an indirect method for controlling child labor. Senator Atlee Pomerene (D-OH) proposed to levy a 10% tax "on the annual net profits of industries" that employed children in violation of certain age and hours standards.[12] The tax penalty would offset any competitive advantage that child labor might otherwise provide. Although the measure was in reality child labor legislation, it was hoped that it might secure Court approval. However, the Supreme Court declared the Pomerene Act (child labor tax) of 1919 unconstitutional in May 1922 (*Bailey v. Drexel Furniture Company*, 259 U.S. 20).[13]

In the wake of the *Drexel* case, Samuel Gompers met at AFL headquarters with Florence Kelley of the National Consumers League, representatives of the NCLC, and others. After extended discussion and a weighing of options, the group developed a proposal for a constitutional amendment to grant Congress the right "to limit, regulate, and prohibit the labor of persons under 18 years of age." The child labor amendment (1924) involved far more than the mere passing of legislation since the case for approval had to be made to each state legislature. While the proponents of child labor reform began optimistically, support began to erode on a number of fronts for reasons not necessarily associated with child labor per se. The proposed amendment remained unratified in 1937 when Congress turned back to direct legislation with consideration of the Fair Labor Standards Act.[14]

---

[10] Grace Abbott, "Federal Regulation of Child Labor, 1906-1938," *The Social Service Review*, September 1939, p. 411. (Hereafter cited as Abbott, *Federal Regulation of Child Labor*.)

[11] Trattner, *Crusade for the Children*, pp. 119-138. See also Edward Keating, *The Gentleman from Colorado: A Memoir* (Denver: Sage Books, 1964), pp. 349-355; Lawrence R. Berger, and S. Ryan Johannson, "Child Health in the Workplace: The Supreme Court in *Hammer v. Dagenhart* (1918)," *Journal of Health Politics, Policy and Law*, spring 1980, pp. 81-97; Arden J. Lea, "Cotton Textiles and the Federal Child Labor Act of 1916," *Labor History*, fall 1975, pp. 485-494; and Walter I. Trattner, "The First Federal Child Labor Law (1916)," *Social Science Quarterly*, December 1969, pp. 507-524.

[12] Abbott, *Federal Regulation of Child Labor*, p. 416.

[13] Trattner, *Crusade for the Children*, pp. 138-142.

[14] Ibid., pp. 163-186. See also "Now the States Must Act! The Past, the Present and the Future of the Effort to Free American Childhood," *American Federationist*, July 1924, pp. 541-553—the AFL journal of which Gompers was editor; Vincent A. McQuade, *The American Catholic Attitude on Child Labor Since 1891* (Washington: The Catholic University of America, 1938), pp. 79-100, and 112-128; Thomas R. Green, "The Catholic Committee for the Ratification of the Child Labor Amendment, 1935-1937: Origin and Limits," *The Catholic Historical Review*, April (continued...)

Early New Deal Enactments (1933-1937)

From the period of the Beveridge bill (1906) to the New Deal era, children's advocates remained divided over the means for ending oppressive child labor. The reform community initially split with respect to federal action. Then, it had largely coalesced behind the Owen-Keating (1916) and Pomerene (1918) bills, debating long and hard over the wisdom of a constitutional amendment (1924). By late 1932, leaders of the Children's Bureau in the Department of Labor (DOL) and the NCLC, with others, decided to shift their focus away from ratification of the constitutional amendment (which was then perceived to be in doubt) and back toward action by individual states.

In retrospect, this shift of emphasis may have been a misreading of the times. "By 1933," notes Walter Trattner in his reform-oriented study, *Crusade for the Children*, "the spreading contagion of child labor had found every weakness and loophole in state labor legislation." He observes: "Sweatshops and fly-by-night plants were exploiting children for little or no pay, moving at will across state lines to take advantage of laws of nearby states. The individual states were unable to halt these abuses which had far-reaching effects, including the complete breakdown of wage scales." Thus, in competitive terms, some argued, it was not feasible for individual states to lead in labor-related reform, even were they predisposed to do so. Trattner concludes: "Everywhere people were looking to Washington for help and direction."[15]

Soon after the inauguration of President Franklin D. Roosevelt in 1933, Congress passed the National Industrial Recovery Act (NIRA, 1933). Under the National Recovery Administration (NRA), industries were encouraged to develop codes of fair competition, which in many instances came to include minimum wage and overtime pay standards, a ban on industrial homework, and the restriction or elimination of child labor. Elimination of child labor under the Cotton Textile Code seemed, momentarily, a major breakthrough. However, in May 1935, the Supreme Court declared that the NIRA was unconstitutional (*Schechter Poultry Corp. et al. v. United States*, 295 U.S. 495).[16]

The Agricultural Adjustment Act (AAA) of May 1933 and the Jones-Costigan Sugar Stabilization Act (1934) were roughly companion measures to the NIRA. In exchange for certain price supports, the government required grower/producer adherence to certain labor and marketing standards.[17] In 1937, the AAA was similarly declared unconstitutional.

In an effort to salvage NIRA and AAA labor standards, less comprehensive measures followed. First, Labor Secretary Frances Perkins, long a child labor reformer, urged that government, as a

---

(...continued)

1988, pp. 248-269; and Richard B. Sherman, "The Rejection of the Child Labor Amendment," *Mid-America: An Historical Review*, January 1963, pp. 3-17. Sherman analyzes the various factors that contributed to the defeat of the child labor campaign during the 1920s.

[15] Trattner, *Crusade for the Children*, p. 189. See also Irwin Yellowitz, "The Origins of Unemployment Reform," *Labor History*, fall 1968, pp. 354-355.

[16] Margaret H. Schoenfeld, "Analysis of the Labor Provisions of the N.R.A. Codes," *Monthly Labor Review*, March 1935, pp. 591-595; Ella Arvilla Merritt, "Trend of Child Labor, 1927-1936," *Monthly Labor Review*, December 1937, pp. 1371-1390.

[17] Trattner, *Crusade for the Children*, pp. 209-210; Fred Greenbaum, *Fighting Progressive: A Biography of Edward P. Costigan*, (Washington: Public Affairs Press, 1971), pp. 143-154; and Stuart Jamieson, *Labor Unionism in American Agriculture*, Washington, U.S. Department of Agriculture, Bulletin No. 836, June 1945, pp. 243-244.

consumer (a more likely constitutional strategy), refuse to purchase items produced by child labor or under unsafe and unclean conditions in tenements (industrial homework). These restrictions were made part of the Public Contracts Act (1936), co-sponsored by Senator David Walsh (D-MA) and Representative Arthur Healey (D-MA), also called the Walsh-Healey Act.[18] Second, agricultural labor standards, though limited, reemerged in the Beet Sugar Act (1937), again linked to a federal support system.[19]

The FLSA and General Child Labor Regulation (1938)

Following the adoption of the Walsh-Healey Act, Secretary Perkins urged passage of general federal minimum wage and overtime pay legislation. Trattner notes that Roosevelt, possibly believing that the wage and hour measure could more easily be enacted "if it were made more attractive by integrating it with child labor," combined the several provisions.[20] Perkins recalls that child labor provisions were added late in the process at the urging of Grace Abbott, who was then head of the Children's Bureau at DOL. "The President readily agreed and was delighted that we might make this bill cover child labor as well as low wages and long hours."[21] After exhaustive debate, the Fair Labor Standards Act (FLSA), with its child labor provisions, became federal law during the summer of 1938.[22]

The FLSA was not a complete victory for advocates of child labor regulation. Historian Jeremy Felt argues that the act may have served "as a deterrent and as an educational force" but added that "in those areas where children are useful they continue to be employed."[23] Further, the act did not address the competition from goods produced abroad by child workers under conditions the FLSA proscribed in America.

During the early 1940s, as enforcement of the FLSA commenced, DOL found (like reformers early in the century) that illegal exploitation of children as laborers was extremely difficult to eradicate where industrial homework persisted. Attempts to regulate the latter were largely unproductive. By the mid-1940s, DOL had imposed an outright ban on industrial homework in certain garment-related fields. Thereafter, abusive child labor seems to have faded as a public policy issue, gradually being replaced by concern with youth unemployment, training, and "school-to-work" transition.[24]

---

[18] Herbert C. Morton, *Public Contracts and Private Wages: Experience Under the Walsh-Healey Act* (Washington: The Brookings Institution, 1965), pp. 14-15, and 23-24. Where government efforts to regulate private sector labor standards had often been disallowed by the courts, setting standards for itself as a consumer had been more successful.

[19] Concerning constitutional issues of this period, see John W. Chambers, "The Big Switch: Justice Roberts and the Minimum-Wage Cases," *Labor History*, winter 1969, pp. 44-73.

[20] Trattner, *Crusade for the Children*, p. 203. See also Storrs, *Civilizing Capitalism*, p. 334.

[21] Frances Perkins, *The Roosevelt I Knew* (New York: The Viking Press, 1946), p. 257.

[22] Although child labor concerns were voiced during debate on the wage/hour legislation, separate hearings were held on that issue. See U.S. Congress, Senate Committee on Interstate Commerce, *To Regulate the Products of Child Labor*, 75th Cong., 1st sess., May 12, 18, and 20, 1937, 192 p.

[23] Jeremy P. Felt, "The Child Labor Provisions of the Fair Labor Standards Act," *Labor History*, fall 1970, pp. 478-479. Jonathan Grossman, then DOL staff historian, similarly notes: "The law avoided some sectors of the work force where most abuses of child labor were concentrated, such as migrant labor, and 'street trades,' such as newspaper venders and shoeshine boys. According to one estimate, only 30,000 child laborers outside of agriculture would be affected." See Jonathan Grossman, "Fair Labor Standards Act of 1938: Maximum Struggle for a Minimum Wage," *Monthly Labor Review*, June 1978, p. 29.

[24] See *GEMSCO, Inc.* v. *Walling*, 324 U.S. 244 (1945).

Child Labor Under the Fair Labor Standards Act

The FLSA, as amended, protects children by setting conditions under which they may be employed and, in certain types of work, prohibiting their employment altogether.[25] Although the basic structure of the act has changed little since 1938, Congress has altered specific provisions of the statute and DOL has variously refined its administration through the rulemaking process.

The Basic Pattern of Coverage

Under the FLSA, employers may not use "oppressive child labor in commerce or in the production of goods for commerce." "Oppressive" is defined in the act and left to the Secretary of Labor to administer. Persons under 18 years of age may not be employed in mining or manufacturing or "in any occupation which the Secretary of Labor shall ... declare to be particularly hazardous for the employment of children ... or detrimental to their health or well-being." Otherwise, 16 years of age is the usual minimum age for employment. The Secretary may permit the employment of persons 14 to 16 years of age in work not deemed "oppressive," that does not interfere with schooling, and that is not detrimental to "health and well-being." The Secretary has established hours during which children of various ages may work.

Exemptions

The Fair Labor Standards Act sets forth general policies and, at the same time, may specify in precise detail, either in the statute or through implementing regulations, how coverage is to be applied: namely, who is covered and who is exempt.[26]

The FLSA, rooted in the commerce clause of the Constitution, excludes from coverage children who are not involved in activities affecting interstate commerce—though such persons may be protected by state statutes. Also excluded are children employed by "a parent or a person standing in place of a parent employing his own child or a child in his custody." A child, for instance, assisting a parent (helping around a "mom-and-pop" corner grocery or doing chores around the home) would not be covered under federal child labor law. Nor do the child labor provisions of the act apply to children employed as actors or in related activities. Traditionally, the "street trades" (such as newspaper delivery) have been regarded as appropriate for children and, thus, are not restrained by FLSA child labor provisions. During the mid-1990s, departmental regulations were altered, administratively, to allow youths of 14 and 15 years of age to work in certain "sports-attending services at professional sporting events."

---

[25] Section 203(l) defines "oppressive child labor." Section 212 defines the relationship of goods produced by child labor with movement in interstate commerce. Section 213(c) sets forth the specialized treatment of child workers under the act and the pattern of exemptions from otherwise standard coverage. The states may (and normally do) have their own child labor laws. While these may supplement the FLSA, they are not necessarily consistent with the FLSA standard. Where there is overlapping coverage, the higher standard (most protective of the youth worker) will normally prevail. When exploring coverage in any particular case, both the state and federal statutes need to be taken into account.

[26] See Title 29 C.F.R. Part 570 for a more complete explanation of child labor regulation in general. In addition, DOL may have issued "opinion letters" that apply a provision of the FLSA to specific workplaces.

Youth and child employment in agriculture is treated somewhat differently from nonagricultural employment.[27] For example, a child working for a parent on a family farm is not covered under the FLSA. The law and regulations include differences with respect to age and the types of work that children and teenagers may perform. **Table 1** provides a general summary of these requirements.

Table 1. Summary of Child Labor Regulation Under the Fair Labor Standards Act

Nonagricultural Employment	Agricultural Employment
Regulations governing youth employment in nonfarm jobs differ somewhat from those pertaining to agricultural employment. In nonfarm work, the permissible jobs and hours of work, by age, are as follows:	In farmwork, permissible jobs and hours of work by age, are as follows:
(1) Persons 18 years or older may perform any job, whether hazardous or not, for unlimited hours;	(1) Youths 16 years and older may perform any job, whether hazardous or not, for unlimited hours;
(2) Youths 16 and 17 years old may perform any nonhazardous job, for unlimited hours; and	(2) Youths 14 and 15 years old may perform any nonhazardous farm job outside of school hours;
(3) Within limits, youths 14 and 15 years old may work in retail stores, food service establishments, and gasoline service stations. They can work no more than 3 hours on a school day, 18 hours in a school week, 8 hours on a nonschool day, or 40 hours in a nonschool week. Work may not begin before 7 a.m. or end after 7 p.m., except from June 1 through Labor Day, when evening hours are extended to 9 p.m.	(3) Youths 12 and 13 years old may work outside of school hours in nonhazardous jobs, either with a parent's written consent or on the same farm as the parent(s);
	(4) Youths under 12 years old may perform jobs on farms owned or operated by a parent, or with a parent's written consent, outside of school hours in nonhazardous jobs on farms not covered by minimum wage requirements.[a]
Fourteen is the minimum age for most nonfarm work. However, at any age, youth may deliver newspapers; perform in radio, television, movie, or theatrical productions; work for a parent in a nonfarm business (except in mining, manufacturing, or hazardous occupations); or, gather evergreens and make evergreen wreaths.	Children of any age are allowed to work on a farm owned or operated by a parent.

Source: Material in this table has been excerpted from the *Handy Reference Guide to the Fair Labor Standards Act*, published by the U.S. Department of Labor, Employment Standards Administration, Wage and Hour Division, WH Publication 1282, Revised October 1996. See Title 29 C.F.R, Part 570, for a more complete explanation of child labor regulation.

a. The "not covered by minimum wage" provision limits the exemption, effectively, to small farms.

Hazardous Occupations Orders

Under the FLSA, manufacturing and mining work is deemed too hazardous for persons under 18 years of age. However, the Secretary may, at his or her discretion, designate other types of work as similarly too hazardous for persons under 18. In such cases, the Secretary will issue

---

[27] The Department of Labor estimates that, during the late 1990s, about 7% of all farmworkers were between 14 and 17 years of age: that is, about 126,000 children in that age group were employed on American farms. However, an unknown number of youth younger than 14 years of age are also employed in agriculture. See U.S. Department of Labor, *Report on the Youth Labor Force*, pp. 52-53.

"hazardous occupations orders" or HOs which are incorporated in the Code of Federal Regulations (see **Table 2**).

Table 2. Hazardous Occupations Orders Issued by the Secretary of Labor: Work Generally Unsuitable for Certain Young Persons

C.F.R.	Type of Work
HO 1 (29 C.F.R. §570.51)	Occupations in or about plants or establishments manufacturing or storing explosives or articles containing explosive components.
HO 2 (29 C.F.R. §570.52)	Occupations of motor-vehicle driver and outside helper.
HO 3 (29 C.F.R. §570.53)	Coal mine occupations.
HO 4 (29 C.F.R. §570.54)	Forest fire fighting and forest fire prevention occupations, timber tract occupations, forestry service occupations, logging occupations, and occupations in the operation of any sawmill, lath mill, shingle mill, or cooperage stock mill.
HO 5 (29 C.F.R. §570.55)	Occupations involved in the operation of power-driven wood-working machines.
HO 6 (29 C.F.R. §570.56)	Exposure to radioactive substances and to ionizing radiations.
HO 7 (29 C.F.R. §570.58)	Occupations involved in the operation of power-driven hoisting apparatus.
HO 8 (29 C.F.R. §570.59)	Occupations involved in the operations of power-driven metal forming, punching, and shearing machines.
HO 9 (29 C.F.R. §570.60)	Occupations in connection with mining, other than coal.
HO 10 (29 C.F.R. §570.61)	Occupations in the operation of power-driven meat-processing machines and occupations involving slaughtering, meat and poultry packing, processing, or rendering.
HO 11 (29 C.F.R. §570.62)	Occupations involved in the operation of bakery machines.
HO 12 (29 C.F.R. §570.63)	Occupations involved in the operation of balers, compactors, and paper-products machines.
HO 13 (29 C.F.R. §570.64)	Occupations involved in the manufacture of brick, tile, and kindred products.
HO 14 (29 C.F.R. §570.65)	Occupations involved in the operation of circular saws, band saws, guillotine shears, chain saws, reciprocating saws, wood chippers, and abrasive cutting discs.
HO 15 (29 C.F.R. §570.66)	Occupations involved in wrecking, demolition, and shipbreaking operations.
HO 16 (29 C.F.R. §570.67)	Occupations in roofing operations.
HO 17 (29 C.F.R. §570.68)	Occupations in excavation operations.

Note: Each of these Hazardous Occupation Orders is developed in detail in the Code of Federal Regulations with specific qualifying factors explained. DOL made several changes to the Hazardous Occupation Orders, effective July 29, 2010. U.S. Department of Labor, Wage and Hour Division, "Child Labor Regulations, Orders and Statements of Interpretation," *Federal Register*, vol. 75, May 20, 2010, pp. 28404-28461.

Often, an exception will be made (and written into the HO) with respect to apprentices and student-learners. The regulations make clear that, where there is a conflict between the HOs and any other provision of law, the higher standard prevails. Each HO is precise, frequently responding to problems that have arisen in the workplace. Currently, there are 17 HOs in place with respect to nonagricultural employment and include occupations such as work involving "manufacturing or storing explosives," "operation of power-driven meat-processing machines," "forest fire fighting," and "logging occupations and occupations in the operation of any sawmill."

Eleven HOs have been published with respect to agricultural employment (see **Table 3**).

Table 3. Hazardous Occupations Orders Issued by the Secretary of Labor: Work Unsuitable for Young Persons Under 16 Years of Age Employed in Agriculture

Order Number	Type of Work
HOA 1	Operating a tractor of over 20 horsepower, or connecting or disconnecting an implement or any of its parts to or from such a tractor.
HOA 2	Operating or assisting to operate (including starting, stopping, adjusting, feeding, or any other activity involving physical contact associated with the operation) any of the following machines: Corn picker, cotton picker, grain combine, hay mower, forage harvester, hay baler, potato digger, or mobile pea viner; Feed grinder, crop dryer, forage blower, auger conveyor, or the unloading mechanism of a nongravity-type self-unloading wagon or trailer; or Power post-hole digger, power post driver, or nonwalking type rotary tiller.
HOA 3	Operating or assisting to operate (including starting, stopping, adjusting, feeding, or any other activity involving physical contact associated with the operation) any of the following machines: Trencher or earthmoving equipment; Fork lift; Potato combine; or Power-driven circular, band, or chain saw.
HOA 4	Working on a farm in a yard, pen, or stall occupied by a: Bull, boar, or stud horse maintained for breeding purposes; or Sow with suckling pigs, or cow with newborn calf (with umbilical cord present).
HOA 5	Felling, bucking, skidding, loading, or unloading timber with a diameter of more than 6 inches.
HOA 6	Working from a ladder or scaffold (e.g., painting, repairing, or building structures, pruning trees, or picking fruit) at a height of over 20 feet.
HOA 7	Driving a bus, truck, or automobile when transporting passengers, or riding on a tractor as a passenger or helper.
HOA 8	Working inside: A fruit, forage, or grain storage designed to retain an oxygen deficient or toxic atmosphere; An upright silo within two weeks after silage has been added or when a top unloading device is in the operating position; A manure pit; or A horizontal silo while operating a tractor for packing purposes.
HOA 9	Handling or applying (including cleaning or decontaminating equipment, disposal or return of empty containers, or serving as a flagman for aircraft applying) agricultural chemicals classified toxic, identified by the word "poison" and the "skull and crossbones" on the label, or identified by the word "warning" on the label.
HOA 10	Handling or using a blasting agent, including but not limited to, dynamite, black powder, sensitized ammonium nitrate, blasting caps, and primer cord.
HOA 11	Transporting, transferring, or applying anhydrous ammonia.

Source: 29 C.F.R. Parts 570-571.

On September 2, 2011, DOL issued a proposed rule to change the regulations that implement the child labor provisions in agriculture. The proposed rule would have modified and expanded the number of hazardous occupations in agriculture. In response to concerns about the potential effects of the proposed rule on the parental exemption, DOL announced, on February 1, 2012, that it was going to reconsider the part of the rule dealing with the interpretation of the parental exemption.[28] On April 26, 2012, DOL announced that it was withdrawing the proposed rule.[29]

Enforcement

Child labor law is enforced by the Wage and Hour Division (WHD) of the U.S. Department of Labor. Much enforcement is complaint driven. Child advocates argue that child workers may not be likely to complain. If children are employed illegally with parental knowledge or consent, complaints may be infrequent. Enforcement may be complicated in the case of migrant farmworkers.

In addition to WHD enforcement, some have urged other forms of nonparental oversight of child labor. Academic problems or frequent truancy could indicate oppressive child labor. Physicians may detect health problems that could be work-related. Efforts in these directions, early in the century, were often unsuccessful but systems of work permits—sometimes linking school attendance and performance to employment—continue to be urged, together with work injury reporting.

Penalties

Employers who illegally employ child workers are subject to both criminal and civil penalties. An employer who willfully violates child labor law is subject to a criminal fine of up to $10,000. For a second conviction of a willful violation, an employer is subject to a fine of up to $10,000, a sentence of up to six months in prison, or both.[30]

Effective June 1, 2010, DOL increased the minimum fines that can be imposed against employers who illegally employ children under the age of 14. For employers who illegally employ a worker under the age of 12, the minimum penalty for violating child labor law was raised to $8,000 per minor (from $850 for nonagricultural employers and $1,150 for agricultural employers). The penalty for illegally employing persons ages 12 or 13 was raised to a minimum of $6,000 per employee (from $850 for nonagricultural employers and $1,025 for agricultural employers). The maximum penalty for illegally employing children under the age of 14 is $11,000 per minor.[31]

---

[28] U.S. Department of Labor, Wage and Hour Division, *U.S. Labor Department to Re-Propose 'Parental Exemption' of Child Labor in Agriculture Rule*, February 1, 2012, http://www.dol.gov/opa/media/press/whd/WHD20120203 htm.

[29] U.S. Department of Labor, Wage and Hour Division, *Labor Department Statement on Withdrawal of Proposed Rule Dealing With Children Who Work in Agricultural Vocations,* http://www.dol.gov/opa/media/press/whd/WHD20120826 htm.

[30] 29 CFR §570.140.

[31] For more detail on civil monetary penalties, see U.S. Department of Labor, Wage and Hour Division, *Initial Civil Money Penalty Assessment Amounts by Violation (Agriculture) as Per 29 CFR §579.5*, June 2010; and U.S. Department of Labor, Wage and Hour Division, *Initial Civil Money Penalty Assessment Amounts by Violation (Non-Agriculture) as Per 29 CFR §579.5*, June 2010.

A civil penalty of up to $50,000 may be assessed for each child labor violation that causes the serious injury or death of a minor. This penalty may be doubled, up to $100,000, if the violations are determined to be willful or repeated.[32]

Re-emergence of the Child Labor Issue (1982-2000)

By the late 1940s, exploitation and endangerment of young children in the world-of-work was popularly believed to have been resolved through legislation (the FLSA) and through the administrative discretion of the Secretary of Labor in implementing the FLSA. But, occasionally someone would recall that very young children still toiled in field harvest work, or an especially egregious accident would bring the more general issue back to the front page.

At the same time, there had begun a gradual shift of focus to a new issue—inadequate opportunities for youth employment—and the related question of delinquency. In May 1961, for example, some 500 men and women met in Washington, DC, "to discuss [this] ... serious but little known national problem." The summary report of the conference observed that

> Again and again in the past decade, juvenile delinquency and the outbreaks of youthful street gangs have made headlines. The fact that large numbers of our youth, 16 to 21 years of age, are out of school and unemployed, significant as it may be in terms of delinquency, has far greater significance in terms of what changes are taking place in our society....

The summary report pointed to an unemployment rate of 17.1% for this age group—with a somewhat higher rate for minority youth. "There have always been young people who dropped out before finishing high school or grade school.... But until recently, except during the depression, there were ample unskilled jobs for workers of limited education." That, the report stated, was no longer true. "When no work is to be had at home, the small-town boys and the farm boys go off to the cities where, ill-prepared for urban jobs, they swell the ranks of the young unemployed." And that, argued Harvard's James B. Conant, "is *social dynamite*" (emphasis in the original).[33]

Through the next two decades, the literature on youth employment (youth joblessness) grew rapidly with numerous panaceas for the problem being advanced. In retrospect, there seems to have been little agreement among policy analysts—except that the problem was serious.[34] However, youth unemployment (or joblessness) notwithstanding, large numbers of youths have continued to seek and to find work.

---

[32] 29 CFR §579.1.

[33] National Committee for Children and Youth, *Social Dynamite: The Report of the Conference on Unemployed, Out-of-School Youth in Urban Areas*, May 24-26, 1961, Washington DC, 1961, pp. 1-2.

[34] The article, "To Be Young, Black and Out of Work," *The New York Times Magazine*, October 23, 1977, p. 39, stated: "Nearly half of all minority youths between 16 and 19 who are in the work force are unemployed." Similarly, *The AFL-CIO American Federationist*, January 1978, p. 1, in an article by Barbara Becnel, "Black Workers: Progress Derailed," observed that unemployment rates "for black teenagers have reached catastrophic levels. In 1976 they averaged 39.2 percent, and in July 1977 they reached an all-time recorded high of 45.5 percent." See U.S. Congress, Joint Economic Committee, *Youth Unemployment*, hearing, 94th Cong., 2nd sess., September 9, 1976 (Washington: GPO, 1977), 130 p.; and U.S. Congress, Senate Committee on the Budget, *Youth Unemployment*, hearing, 95th Cong., 2nd sess., February 17, 1978 (Washington: GPO, 1978), 136 p.

Although many young persons under the age of 15 are employed, there are more data on the employment status of older youth.[35] Looking at the labor force participation of 15- to 17-year-old youth through the period 1996-1998, on average, "about a fourth of both male and female youths were employed during average school months. During the summer, about one-third of both male and female youths worked," the Department of Labor reported. But DOL also reported significant variations in employment status when considered in terms of race and ethnicity. About 28% of white youths were employed during school months; about 38% during the summer. For blacks, the comparable figures were 13% (school months) and 20% (summer); for youth of Hispanic origin, 15% (school months) and 20% (summer).[36]

The Reagan-Era Initiatives

In July 1982, Labor Secretary Raymond Donovan (for the Reagan Administration) proposed that existing child labor policy be updated. The Administration's plan would have (1) opened more opportunities for employment for children 14 and 15 years of age; (2) extended the number of hours per day and per week that children might be employed; (3) revised standards for the employment of child workers in jobs once considered too hazardous; and (4) simplified and broadened the manner in which employers could become certified by DOL to employ full-time students at less than the standard minimum wage.

The Donovan proposal sparked an immediate reaction. When opening hearings before the House Labor Standards Subcommittee of which he was chair, Representative George Miller (D-CA) sharply criticized the Administration's proposals.[37] In turn, Wage/Hour Administrator William Otter defended them as sound and reasonable public policy. He read from letters from young persons, parents, and potential employers urging flexibility in child labor regulation so that 14- and 15-year-olds could be more easily employed. Although acknowledging a high unemployment rate among 16- to 19-year-olds, Otter affirmed his concern "about the unemployment levels of all age groups" and stated the view that "[u]nreasonable and artificial impediments to the employment of all age groups should be eliminated."[38]

Proponents and critics seemed to agree that the Reagan Administration "had walked into a minefield" where the child labor issue was concerned.[39] In February 1983, *Nation's Restaurant News* reported that "Federal wage and hour regulators are sifting through a blizzard of letters from restaurant operators across the nation supporting the Reagan Administration's plan to relax

---

[35] The Current Population Survey (CPS), which is the source of the national monthly unemployment rate, collects data on the labor force status of persons ages 16 and over. The CPS is a household survey conducted for the Bureau of Labor Statistics (BLS) by the U.S. Census Bureau; U.S. Department of Labor, Bureau of Labor Statistics, *Labor Force Statistics from the Current Population Survey*, available at http://stats.bls.gov/cps/home htm. The National Longitudinal Surveys, a series of household surveys sponsored by BLS, collect data on the labor market activity of younger persons; U.S. Department of Labor, Bureau of Labor Statistics, *National Longitudinal Surveys*, available at http://www.bls.gov/nls/. In their article, "Illegal Child Labor in the United States: Prevalence and Characteristics" (*Industrial and Labor Relations Review*, October 2000, pp. 17-40), Douglas L. Kruse and Douglas Mahony evaluate currently available data on workers under 15 years of age.

[36] U.S. Department of Labor, *Report on the Youth Labor Force*, updated November 2000, pp. 30-31. Hispanics are included in both black and white data sets. Data are pooled across a three-year period.

[37] Press release from Congressman George Miller, July 27, 1982.

[38] U.S. Congress, House Committee on Education and Labor, Subcommittee on Labor Standards, *Oversight Hearings— Proposed Changes in Child Labor Regulations*, hearing, 97th Cong., 2nd sess., July 28, and August 3, 1982, pp. 1-30.

[39] Peter Edelman, "Child Labor Revisited," *The Nation*, August 21-28, 1982, p. 136.

---

child labor restrictions on the employment of young teenagers in food-service outlets." But, the *News* also reported that the proposal had "generated a storm of protest from educational groups, labor unions, and Congressmen who expressed outrage over what some described as a scheme to enable restauranteurs to exploit school age workers."[40]

For a time, the regulations remained under review with periodic speculation that their release was imminent. In the spring of 1984, the *Nation's Restaurant News* speculated that they would likely appear "by the end of the year."[41] Later, it was reported that the proposal was "likely to resurface" in the near future.[42] But, after a year, it was noted that DOL was again delaying "action on a regulation governing the employment of minors between the ages of 14 and 16."[43] Some suggested "a politically inspired delay" in release of a final rule.[44] Whatever the cause, a final revision never appeared.

Controversies and Changes of Law

As the Reagan Administration proposals receded ever further into the background, several committees of Congress conducted hearings on aspects of child labor—a process that would continue, intermittently, through the 1980s and 1990s. But, although they established an evidentiary record, no general legislation restructuring child labor law was approved.

In 1987, Labor Secretary William Brock announced the formation of a Child Labor Advisory Committee to assist him with interpretation of child labor issues. The committee was chaired by Linda Golodner, who was also executive director of the National Consumers' League. The advisory body quickly concluded that child labor was "often on the low end of the priority list" at DOL and that it took "very, very long for [its] ... recommendations to get through the bureaucracy." In the spring of 1989, the department explained that the suggestions of the committee had, gradually, moved through four lower levels of review and that, by mid-May, they had reached the desk of the Administrator of the Wage and Hour Division.[45]

Administrative changes in the wake of the 1988 election may have caused further delay in moving forward with child labor issues. With the appointment of Elizabeth Dole as Secretary of Labor (January 1989), the department appeared to have adopted a more active interest in the child labor issue. In mid-1989, Secretary Dole announced the appointment of William Brooks of General Motors to serve as Assistant Secretary for Employment Standards and charged him, inter alia, with child labor issues.[46]

---

[40] *Nation's Restaurant News*, February 28, 1983, p. 2.

[41] Bureau of National Affairs, *Daily Labor Report*, April 23, 1984, p. A7.

[42] Ken Rankin, "Pols May Pull Child Labor Scheme off Back Burner," *Nation's Restaurant News*, November 26, 1984, p. 9.

[43] Bureau of National Affairs, *Daily Labor Report*, April 30, 1985, p. A9.

[44] Joseph A. Walsh, "Teen-Age Work Rules Targeted Again," *UA Journal*, September 1982, p. 4.

[45] Bureau of National Affairs, *Daily Labor Report*, May 18, 1989, pp. A10-A11. The Committee had addressed such issues as "door-to-door" sales by persons 14 to 15 years of age, a special overtime exemption for "bat boys," and work around commercial paper balers. It also examined the structure of penalties for child labor violations. During this period, GAO was looking into some of these same issues while the National Consumers' League launched its own independent review of child labor practices.

[46] Bureau of National Affairs, *Daily Labor Report*, July 31, 1989, pp. A6-A7; and August 30, 1989, pp. A7-A8.

Almost at once, the new assistant secretary was confronted with a GAO report affirming that child labor violations had increased dramatically during recent years. But GAO also suggested that data concerning work (and injuries) involving young persons were not entirely satisfactory. A more nearly adequate database was needed.[47]

Departmental initiatives, with investigations by GAO and the Consumers' League, combined with existing congressional concern to give the issue of child labor enhanced visibility. In early 1990, Brooks informed the Advisory Committee that a special task force on child labor would be formed within DOL and would look into such issues as possible revision of the hazardous work orders and the penalty structure for child labor violations. Brooks promised, the *Daily Labor Report* reported, "that in the next six months, rigorous enforcement of child labor law will be the watchword of the agency."[48] Hearings followed, along with new legislative proposals. And, DOL launched *Operation Child Watch,* the first in a series of "sweeps" or general inspections aimed at compliance.[49] Changes were made in the penalty structure and, presumably, in DOL's enforcement policy.

Some viewed DOL's initiatives as a "commendable start"—but there were also misgivings. Representative Don Pease (D-OH), one of the more outspoken advocates of child labor reform, argued that something more was needed than "occasional public relations events" and intermittent crack-downs on violators. Although Pease seems to have favored legislative reform, the Bush Administration apparently did not.[50] In June 1990, Brooks assured the National Grocers Association that no new legislation was necessary: that any needed changes "can be made administratively."[51] The status of the Advisory Committee was unclear. Golodner reported in November of 1990 that no meeting of the committee had been held since early in the year, that the terms of current members had expired in March, and that no new members had been named by DOL. In late 1990, Secretary Dole indicated her intent to retire. Brooks resigned to return to General Motors.[52]

In 1994, the Clinton Administration proposed a general review of child labor regulation, similar in scope to that proposed by Secretary Donovan, though of a different thrust. Comprehensive oversight and administrative reform continued to be discussed but, essentially, both Congress and DOL proceeded on an ad hoc basis.

The "Bat Boy" Issue

In April 1986, Senator Dan Quayle (R-IN) proposed that child labor law be relaxed to permit 14- and 15-year-olds to work as bat boys or bat girls for professional baseball teams, even when games might run until late at night. The Senator stated that baseball "is the All-American sport" and indicated that youngsters should not be forced to wait until they were 16 years of age "to

---

[47] Bureau of National Affairs, *Daily Labor Report*, November 22, 1989, pp. A7-A8.

[48] Bureau of National Affairs, *Daily Labor Report*, February 8, 1990, pp. A10-A12.

[49] Bureau of National Affairs, *Daily Labor Report*, March 19, 1990, pp. A16-A17; May 1, 1990, p. A11; and June 26, 1990, pp. A8-A9.

[50] Bureau of National Affairs, *Daily Labor Report*, May 4, 1990, pp. A13-A15.

[51] Bureau of National Affairs, *Daily Labor Report*, June 25, 1990, p. A8.

[52] Bureau of National Affairs, *Daily Labor Report*, November 5, 1990, pp. A6-A7; and November 13, 1990, p. A6.

associate with the players of their home town teams."[53] Congress mandated a study of the question, and the issue was allowed to die.

In the spring of 1993, the matter was raised again when it prevented a 14-year-old youngster from Georgia from serving as a bat boy for the Savannah Cardinals. Labor Secretary Robert Reich, faced with the difficulty of explaining the logic of the work hours requirement, suspended its enforcement and proposed to allow children of 14 and 15 years of age to work as late as circumstances might dictate—"before, during, and after a sporting event," around the playing field, "club house or locker room"—to provide "sports-attending services at professional sporting events." Certain conditions were specified, intended to protect children from hazardous activity. And thus, by the spring of 1995, the regulation had been changed.[54]

But questions remained. For example, if it were inappropriate, per se, for young persons (14 and 15 years of age) to work late hours on a school night, did it really matter what sort of work they were doing? How did "sports-attending services" differ, in that context, from work in the food services industry or in a real estate or law office entering data into a computer? Might a more routine business environment be preferable to that of professional sports for the education and welfare of 14- and 15-year-olds? Some in the restaurant industry argued that "it was unfair to exempt the sports industry from the hours and time restrictions while leaving the restrictions in place for all other employment."[55]

Paper Balers and Compactors

Under Hazardous Occupations Order No. 12, persons under 18 were not allowed to load waste paper and boxes into commercial (industrial) paper balers and compactors. Operation of such equipment, DOL had determined, was especially hazardous for younger workers. Even loading them was viewed by the department as a serious risk. Karen Keesling, Acting Administrator of DOL's Wage and Hour Division, explained that it was not just the loading but that individuals involved in that process would likely reach into a baler or compactor to keep the materials from falling out or to clear jammed materials—and "that is extremely hazardous."[56] Conversely, the National Grocers Association termed HO 12 "a prime example of regulatory excess."[57]

In March 1995, Representative Thomas Ewing (R-IL) introduced H.R. 1114, legislation that would have permitted operation of the baling/compacting machinery by "minors under 18 years of age"—so long as the equipment met safety standards established by the private sector American National Standards Institute (ANSI). A similar proposal was introduced by Senator Larry Craig (R-ID). The legislation was supported by the National Grocers Association and opposed by the Child Labor Coalition (a youth advocacy group) and by people in the trade union movement. As signed into law (P.L. 104-174) on August 6, 1996, the legislation had been redrawn to permit workers "who are 16 and 17 years of age ... to load materials into, but not operate or unload materials from, scrap paper balers and paper box compactors" that meet ANSI safety

---

[53] *Congressional Record*, April 9, 1986, p. S9013.

[54] *Federal Register*, May 13, 1994, p. 25167; and April 17, 1995, pp. 19336-19337. The basis for the decision is explained by Robert B. Reich in his account, *Locked in the Cabinet* (New York: Alfred A. Knopf, 1997), pp. 113-116.

[55] *Federal Register*, April 17, 1995, p. 19337.

[56] Letter from Karen Keesling to Ronald A. Block (attorney for the National Grocers Association), October 16, 1992.

[57] Statement of Thomas F. Wenning, Senior Vice President and General Counsel, National Grocers Association (NGA), July 11, 1995, House Subcommittee on Workforce Protection.

standards and where certain other requirements have been met. Whether the qualifying language was adequate to protect the youthful workers, however, remained in dispute.[58]

Work-Related Operation of Motor Vehicles

Hazardous Occupations Order No. 2, as developed at the discretion of the Secretary of Labor, restricted the work-related operation of certain motor vehicles by persons under the age of 18 as "particularly hazardous" for younger workers. While not absolutely precluded, strict guidelines and limitations had to be complied with. Conformity with specified safety standards and operation only during daylight hours was required. Employment-related driving could only be "occasional and incidental" though there might be some doubt about the definition of such terms.

In April 1994, Representative Mike Kreidler (D-WA) introduced legislation directing the Secretary to modify HO 2 to permit a wider opportunity for young persons to drive in conjunction with their regular work. No action was taken on the Kreidler bill and in July 1995, new legislation was introduced by Representative Randy Tate (R-WA) and Senator Slade Gorton (R-WA). Hearings followed but the legislation died at the close of the 104th Congress. In July 1997, Representative Larry Combest (R-TX) reintroduced the issue as H.R. 2327 (the Drive for Teen Employment Act).

Though modification of HO 2 had been endorsed by automobile dealers, it had been opposed by the Department of Labor and by groups associated with children's advocacy such as the Child Labor Coalition and the National Consumers League. Persons 16 and 17 years of age, normally, are beginning drivers who will have only recently qualified for a driver's license. Although some youngsters may be fine drivers, it was argued that their lack of experience created a significant risk, both to the young persons themselves and to the public.

In its final form, the legislation proposed to allow persons 17 years of age to engage in limited professional driving, under specified safety conditions and with certain limitations, but would still prohibit such activity by persons under 17. The Combest bill, as amended, was signed by President Clinton on October 31, 1998 (P.L. 105-334).[59]

---

[58] *Congressional Record*, May 2, 1995, pp. S6009-S6010; October 24, 1995, pp. H10661-H10667; and July 16, 1996, pp. S7912-S7914. See also U.S. Congress, House Committee on Economic and Educational Opportunities, *Authority for 16 and 17 Year Olds to Load Materials into Balers and Compactors*, report to accompany H.R. 1114, 104th Cong., 1st sess., H.Rept. 104-278 (Washington: GPO, 1995).

[59] CRS Report 98-561, *Child Labor in Hazardous Occupations: "On-the-Job Driving" by Youth Workers*, by William G. Whittaker (available upon request).

Child Labor Legislation

The remainder of this report summarizes child labor legislation in recent Congresses, beginning with the most recent Congress and ending with the 108th Congress.

The 113th Congress

The CARE Act of 2013

On June 12, 2013, Representative Lucille Roybal-Allard (D-CA) introduced H.R. 2342, the Children's Act for Responsible Employment of 2013, or CARE Act of 2013. Among other things, H.R. 2342 would raise from 14 to 16 the minimum age at which youth may be employed in agriculture. The act would raise from 16 to 18 the minimum age at which youth employed in agriculture can work in occupations declared hazardous by the Secretary of Labor.

Under current law, the minimum age at which youth can be employed in nonagricultural occupations is 16. The minimum age to be employed in agricultural occupations is 14. H.R. 2342 would raise the minimum age to be employed in agricultural occupations to 16, the same as in nonagricultural occupations.

Under current law, youth under the age of 18 cannot be employed in nonagricultural occupations found by the Secretary of Labor to be particularly hazardous for the employment of youth. In agriculture, the minimum age to be employed in hazardous occupations is 16. H.R. 2342 would raise the minimum age to work in hazardous occupations in agriculture to 18, the same as in nonagricultural occupations.

H.R. 2342 would not allow the employment of youth in hazardous occupations on a farm owned by a parent. Under current law, the restrictions on the employment of youth in hazardous occupations in agriculture do not apply to a farm owned or operated by a parent. Outside of agriculture, the restrictions on the employment of youth in hazardous occupations apply to all businesses, whether or not owned by a parent.

Under current law, in nonagricultural occupations, except in mining, manufacturing, and hazardous occupations, youth under the age of 16 may work in a business owned by a parent.[60] In agriculture, youth of any age may work on a farm owned or operated by a parent.[61] H.R. 2342 would change the parental exemption in agriculture to a farm owned by a parent, instead of a farm owned or operated by a parent.

---

[60] U.S. Department of Labor, *FLSA Child Labor Rules Advisor*, available at http://www.dol.gov/elaws/esa/flsa/cl/exemptions.asp.

[61] A parent may include a person "standing in place of the parent." A person who stands in place of a parent may include a person who takes a child into his home and treats the child as a member of the family, supporting and educating the child as if the child was his own. 29 C.F.R. §570.126.

According to the DOL *Field Operations Handbook*, a farm is operated by the parent if the parent exerts "active and direct control over the operation of the farm or ranch by making day-to-day decisions affecting basic income, work assignments, hiring and firing of employees and exercising direct supervision of the farm or ranch work." U.S. Department of Labor, Wage and Hour Division, *Field Operations Handbook*, Section 33d03(e), available at http://www.dol.gov/whd/FOH/FOH_Ch33.pdf.

Under current law, youth ages 12 or 13 can be employed on a farm with the consent of the parent or if the parent is employed on the same farm. Also, with the consent of the parent youth under 12 can be employed on a farm that is exempt from the minimum wage standards of the FLSA (i.e., on small farms).[62] H.R. 2342 would remove these exemptions.

H.R. 2342 would direct the Secretary of Labor to revise federal child labor regulations to prohibit the employment of children under the age of 18 in occupations that involve the handling of pesticides.

H.R. 2342 would establish minimum civil penalties and raise the maximum civil penalty for each employee subject to a violation of child labor law. The legislation would establish criminal penalties for repeated or willful violations of child labor law that result in the death or serious injury or illness of an employee under the age of 18.

H.R. 2342 was referred to the Subcommittee on Workforce Protections of the House Education and the Workforce Committee.

The 112th Congress

The CARE Act of 2011

In the 112th Congress, Representative Lucille Roybal-Allard (D-CA) introduced H.R. 2234, the Children's Act for Responsible Employment of 2011, or CARE Act of 2011. The text of H.R. 2234 is the same as H.R. 2342, which was introduced in the 113th Congress and described above. H.R. 2234 was introduced on June 16, 2011, and was referred to the Subcommittee on Workforce Protections of the House Education and the Workforce Committee.

The 111th Congress

The CARE Act of 2009

On September 15, 2009, Representative Lucille Roybal-Allard (D-CA) introduced H.R. 3564, the Children's Act for Responsible Employment of 2009, or CARE Act. The legislation would prohibit the employment of persons under 18 in agriculture, unless they are employed by a parent (or someone standing in the place of a parent) on a farm owned and operated by the parent.

The legislation would also repeal Section 213(c)(4) of the FLSA, which allows the Secretary of Labor to grant requests for waivers from employers to allow them to hire persons ages 10 and 11 to work outside of school hours in the hand harvesting of crops.

The bill would increase civil penalties and establish criminal penalties for violations of child labor law.

---

[62] A farm that does not employ more than 500 "man days" of labor in any calendar quarter in the preceding calendar year is exempt from both the minimum wage and overtime standards of the FLSA for the current calendar year. A "man day" is any day during which an employee performs at least one hour of farm work. U.S. Department of Labor, *Agricultural Employers Under the Fair Labor Standards Act (FLSA)*, available at http://www.dol.gov/whd/regs/ compliance/whdfs12.pdf.

The legislation would direct the Secretary of Labor to analyze data and report annually to Congress on each work-related injury, illness, or death of persons under the age of 18 employed in agriculture. Employers would be required to report to the Secretary of Labor any work-related death or any serious injury or illness of agricultural employees under the age of 18.

The bill would require the Secretary of Labor to issue rules to prohibit the employment of persons under the age of 18 in occupations where workers are protected from exposure to pesticides.

H.R. 3564 was referred to the Subcommittee on Workforce Protections of the House Committee on Education and Labor.

The 110th Congress

Several child labor bills were introduced in the 110th Congress. (**Table 4**, below, provides a summary of this legislation.)

Table 4. Child Labor Proposals in the 110th Congress

Bill No.	Sponsor	Action Beyond Referral	Impact
H.R. 2637	Woolsey	Passed House. Provisions are included in H.R. 493.	Raises the maximum civil penalties for violations of child labor law.
H.R. 2674	Roybal-Allard	None	Focus is on agricultural child workers.
H.R. 6861	Braley	None	Raises the maximum civil penalties and establishes criminal penalties for violations of child labor law.
S. 1598	Coleman	Provisions are included in H.R. 493.	Raises the maximum civil penalties for child labor violations.
S. 1614	Harkin	None	Raises the maximum civil penalties and establishes criminal penalties for violations of child labor law.

The Child Labor Protection Act of 2007

Different bills with same title—the Child Labor Protection Act of 2007—were introduced in the 110th Congress.

In the House, on June 8, 2007, Representative Lynn Woolsey (D-CA) introduced H.R. 2637, the Child Labor Protection Act of 2007. The legislation was referred to the Committee on Education and Labor. The House approved the bill by voice vote on June 12, 2007. H.R. 2637 would increase from $10,000 to $11,000 the maximum employer penalty for each employee who is subject to a violation of the child labor provisions of the FLSA. The measure would also establish a maximum civil penalty of $50,000 for each violation that causes the death or serious injury of any employee under the age of 18. The $50,000 penalty may be doubled for repeated or willful violations of child labor law. The bill would also increase from $1,000 to $1,100 the maximum penalty for violating the minimum wage or overtime provisions of the FLSA.

In the Senate, Senator Norm Coleman (R-MN), on June 12, 2007, introduced S. 1598, which was also called the Child Labor Protection Act of 2007. The measure was referred to the Committee on Health, Education, Labor, and Pensions (HELP). S. 1598 includes the identical changes in civil penalties as contained in H.R. 2637.

On April 23, 2008, Senator Olympia Snowe (R-ME) introduced an amendment (S.Amdt. 4573) in the nature of a substitute to H.R. 493, the Genetic Information Nondiscrimination Act of 2008. H.R. 493 was approved by the House on April 25, 2007. Senator Snowe's amendment included the provisions of H.R. 2637/S. 1598. The Senate approved the amendment by a vote of 95 in favor and none opposed. The measure was signed into law by President George W. Bush on May 21, 2008, and became P.L. 110-233.

On June 13, 2007, Senator Tom Harkin (D-IA) introduced S. 1614, another bill that was called the Child Labor Protection Act of 2007. S. 1614 would amend the FLSA to establish a minimum civil penalty of $500 and a maximum penalty of $15,000 for each employee who is subject to a child labor violation. The bill would also create a minimum penalty of $15,000 and a maximum penalty of $50,000 for each violation of child labor law that causes the death or serious injury of an employee under the age of 18. The latter penalty could be doubled to a maximum of $100,000. The bill would also increase from $1,000 to $1,100 the maximum penalty for violating the minimum wage or overtime provisions of the FLSA. Finally, the measure would establish criminal penalties (fines, imprisonment, or both) for violations of the child labor provisions of the FLSA. The bill was referred to the Senate HELP Committee.

The CARE Act of 2007

On June 12, 2007, Representative Lucille Roybal-Allard (D-CA) introduced H.R. 2674, the Children's Act for Responsible Employment of 2007, or CARE Act of 2007. Except for two provisions, the measure is the same as the CARE Act of 2005 (H.R. 3482), which was introduced in the 109th Congress. Unlike H.R. 3482, the CARE Act of 2007 does not direct the Secretary of Labor to employ additional inspectors to enforce child labor law. Also, the CARE Act of 2007 would not amend the WIA law with respect to youth activities under the Migrant and Seasonal Farmworker Programs.

H.R. 2674 was referred to the Subcommittee on Workforce Protections of the Education and Labor Committee.

The Child Labor Safety Act

Representative Bruce Braley (D-IA) introduced the Child Labor Safety Act. The act would increase from $11,000 to $50,000 the maximum civil penalty for each employee who is subject to a violation of the child labor provisions of the FLSA. The bill would also raise from $50,000 to $100,000 the maximum penalty for each violation that causes the death or serious injury of any employee under the age of 18. The measure would impose criminal penalties (a maximum fine of $50,000 or imprisonment for up to six months) for violations of child labor law. The bill was introduced on September 10, 2008, and was referred to the Committee on Education and Labor.

The 109th Congress

As with previous years, child labor remained a subject of interest among some Members of the 109th Congress. Several bills from prior Congresses were re-introduced. Several new bills were added. (See **Table 5**, below.)

Protecting Child Models

On March 8, 2005, the Child Modeling Exploitation Prevention Act (H.R. 1142) was introduced in the House by Representative Mark Foley (R-FL), with others. The bill was referred to the Subcommittee on Workforce Protections of the House Committee on Education and the Workforce and to the Subcommittee on Crime, Terrorism, and Homeland Security of the House Committee on the Judiciary. No further action was taken on the measure.

For a number of years, Representative Foley had raised the issue of children engaged in modeling on Internet sites. "What occurs," he explained in a floor statement, "... is that young girls, 10, 12, 13 years old, are encouraged by their parents and aided and abetted by individuals to display themselves on the Internet for viewer ship, if you will, [by] people who pay a fee, a monthly fee in order to view the site." Although some parents, he suggested, are deceived into thinking that such activity is legitimate modeling, Mr. Foley disagreed. He stated that he was "not suggesting that there is not an appropriate place in commerce for young people to display their talents" but, rather, that he had in mind a particular type of website that encourages "inappropriate" types of modeling by children.[63]

In the 109th Congress, Representative Foley introduced H.R. 1142, which was similar to legislation introduced in the previous Congress (by Representative Foley in the House and Senator Jim Bunning in the Senate).[64] The proposal amended Section 12 of the FLSA to provide that "no employer may employ a child model in exploitive child modeling." It went on to explain:

> (A) In this subsection, the term 'exploitive child modeling' means modeling involving the use of a child under 17 years old for financial gain without the purpose of marketing a product or service other than the image of the child.
>
> (B) Such term applies to any such use, regardless of whether the employment relationship of the child is direct or indirect, or contractual or noncontractual, or is termed that of an independent contractor.

The measure distinguished between an image that is exploitive and one that, "taken as a whole, has serious literary, artistic, political, or scientific value." The legislation proposed both fines and imprisonment (of not more than 10 years) for violators.

Table 5. Child Labor Proposals in the 109th Congress

Bill No.	Sponsor	Action Beyond Referral	Impact
H.R. 1142	Foley	None	To prohibit "exploitive child modeling" involving persons under 17 years of age
H.R. 2870	Lantos	None	A comprehensive overview of child labor with restrictions placed upon child workers: school-to-work transition; prohibition of youth peddling; mandates for reporting requirements; and imposition of certain other restraints

---

[63] *Congressional Record*, September 18, 2002, pp. H6349-H6350.

[64] This is a general summary of the provisions of H.R. 1142. The reader may want to review the text of the bill for more precision and detail.

Bill No.	Sponsor	Action Beyond Referral	Impact
H.R. 3482	Roybal-Allard	None	Focuses upon agricultural child workers.
H.R. 3753	Musgrave	None	Comprehensive home school bill; suggests that "home schooled students" (14 to 16 years of age) be permitted to work longer than hours worked by public school students
H.R. 4190	DeLauro	None	Requires (a) that the Secretary of Labor not pre-disclose an inspection, and (b) that a study and report of child labor issues be made to Congress
S. 1691	Craig	None	See the Musgrave bill (H.R. 3753), above
S. 2357	Kennedy	None	Comprehensive bill (368 pp.) that refers to the restriction of child labor and enforcement of internationally recognized labor standards dealing with child labor

Young American Workers' Bill of Rights

General restructuring of the child labor components of the FLSA has long been sought, though from somewhat different perspectives, by industry and by labor. In 1990 (the 101st Congress), Representatives Don Pease (D-OH), Charles Schumer (D-NY) and Tom Lantos (D-CA) introduced legislation titled the "Young American Workers' Bill of Rights." With various changes (but with a continuity of thrust), the legislation would be reintroduced in each Congress thereafter.

In the 109th Congress, the initiatives were set forth in H.R. 2870 (Lantos), the Youth Worker Protection Act. The Lantos bill was comprehensive, providing for a wide variety of changes in current law and practice.[65]

> (a) The bill begins by defining a "minor." He or she must be "is at least 14 years old or, if younger than 14 years old, is otherwise permitted to work under this Act." "In the case of a minor who is between the ages of 16 and 18 years, the employment is not in an occupation that is particularly hazardous for the employment of children between those ages or detrimental to their health or well-being.... " "The minor is employed in accordance with this Act and in accordance with any other Federal, State, or local law that provides greater protection to minors."

> (b) The minor has a work permit that includes the specified provisions under this Act.

> —The work permit shall include name, date of birth, gender, racial or ethnic background, and contact information for the minor; name, contact information, and consent of a parent of the minor; a certification (if appropriate) by a school official showing attendance requirements; e.g., name, contact information, and type of business of the employer; and type of work.

> —The Secretary of Labor will prescribe a unified model for such work permits that will contain information concerning the identity of the child worker and his/her parent (or a similar person where appropriate), contact information and parental consent for the child to

---

[65] This is a general summary of the provisions of H.R. 2870. The reader may want to review the text of the bill for more precision and detail.

work, school status, identification of employer, type of work to be engaged in, name and contact information of the designated state agency, summary of age limitations and other legal requirements for employment of minors, among other information. A system of expiration dates for individual work permits is specified.

—The designated state agency may revoke a work permit if the agency finds either of the following: (1) the minor "is not in compliance with school attendance requirements," or (2) the minor is adversely affected by the employment involved. The minor or the parent of the minor would have had an option for appeal of the revocation.

(c) Hours that are allowable for work by minors were specified in H.R. 2870, together with the number of hours per day and week that can be worked.

(d) If the minor sustains a serious work-related injury, the designated state agency must be notified by each of the following: the employer, the appropriate medical professional, the appropriate law enforcement officer (where applicable), and an employee of the school attended by the minor where an absence of more than three days is involved.[66]

(e) The bill provided that the designated state agency must collect and retain (for seven years) statistical data concerning the work permit system and any work-related injury information.

(f) The designated state agency must report annually to the Secretary of Labor. The report shall include assorted statistical data (see item "e" above) and information concerning "the activities and number of work-hours devoted by State and local government employees (including contractors) to the administration and enforcement of child labor laws in the State."

(g) The bill would have provided that "[no employer may employ a minor in youth peddling" and defines what is included in the concept of youth "peddling." (See discussion of the "peddling" issue, above.)

(h) It set forth extensive requirements for enforcement and penalties.

(i) The bill amended Section 13(c) of the FLSA to raise the age for employment in agriculture outside of school hours from "twelve years of age" to "fourteen years of age."

(j) It makes uniform the standard for employment in hazardous agricultural work.

(k) The bill would repeal the provision of current law permitting, at the discretion of the Secretary (with certain specific criteria), children as young as 10 years of age to work in hand harvest agricultural work.

(l) It would eliminate the employment of children under 18 years of age in connection with commercial paper balers and compactors. (See discussion above.)

(m) "Not later than 24 months after the date of the enactment of this section," the Secretary of Labor is directed to promulgate a rule revising the Hazardous Occupations restraints in certain specified industries. The Secretary was also directed at "appropriate intervals, but in

---

[66] A "serious work-related injury" is one that results in "(1) the death of the minor; (2) medical attention for the minor; or (3) investigation by a law enforcement agency."

no case less than once during each five-year period," to conduct "a comprehensive review" of the Hazardous Occupations Orders to assure that they are current.

(n) Within 24 months of enactment of this section, the Secretary is directed to promulgate a rule to prohibit employment of minors in (1) seafood processing and (2) employment "requiring a minor to handle or dispose of oil or other liquids from fryers."

(o) Within 36 months, the Secretary was directed to review the employment of minors in work involving: (1) "[r]epetitive bending, stooping, twisting, or squatting," (2) "[l]ifting of heavy and/or unwieldy objects," (3) "[w]orking alone or late at night in retail establishments where there is direct contact with the public and cash is handled," and (4) "[w]ork in the entertainment industry that is detrimental to the health, safety, education or well-being of minors."[67] The Secretary shall submit to Congress a report of the review, together with proposed regulations governing such work.

On July 25, 2005, H.R. 2870 was referred to the House Subcommittee on Workforce Protections of the House Committee on Education and the Workforce. The subcommittee took no action on the bill.

The CARE Act of 2005

For several years, Representative Lucille Roybal-Allard (D-CA) presented legislation that dealt primarily, though not exclusively, with child labor in agriculture. On July 27, 2005, Representative Roybal-Allard introduced H.R. 3482, the Children's Act for Responsible Employment of 2005, or the CARE Act of 2005.

The Roybal-Allard bill began with a revision of Section 13(c), eliminating the option of having young persons under 16 years of age employed in agriculture "including in an agricultural occupation that the Secretary of Labor finds and declares to be particularly hazardous." The bill offered two exceptions: where the employee "is employed by a parent of the employee or by a person standing in the place of the parent," or "on a farm owned or operated by the parent or person" standing in the place of a parent. Further, the bill repealed Section 213(c)(4), which allows the Secretary of Labor to grant requests for waivers from employers to allow them to hire minors ages 10 and 11 to work outside of school hours in the hand harvesting of crops.[68]

The bill expanded the penalties, both civil and criminal, for persons found to be in violation of the act. Also, the Secretary of Labor, with respect to persons under 18 years of age employed in agriculture, was to gather data with respect to "each serious lost-time work-related injury, serious lost-time worker-related illness," or work-related death. An employer was expected to submit a report to the Secretary. Failure to file a report was subject to a civil penalty of up to $7,000 per violation. The Secretary could employ at least 100 additional inspectors, whose principal purpose would be to enforce compliance with child labor laws.

The bill provided that the Secretary, not later than 180 days after the date of enactment, would issue rules relating to the exposure of child workers to certain pesticides and related chemicals. It

---

[67] Arguably, the latter could include protection of child models. See discussion above.

[68] The U.S. Department of Labor has been enjoined from issuing such waivers. U.S. Department of Labor, *Child Labor Requirements in Agricultural Occupations Under the Fair Labor Standards Act*, Child Labor Bulletin 102, June 2007, available at http://www.dol.gov/whd/regs/compliance/childlabor102.pdf, p. 3.

allowed for some measure of accommodation between the Secretary of Labor and the Administrator of the Environmental Protection Agency with respect to pesticide-related fines.

Finally, H.R. 3482 amended the Workforce Investment Act (WIA) of 1998 to provide the greater of $10 million or 4% of the amount appropriated for WIA youth activities for youth activities under the Migrant and Seasonal Farmworker Programs.

The Roybal-Allard bill was referred to the House Committee on Education and the Workforce. On October 12, 2005, it was referred to the Subcommittee on Workforce Protections and to the Subcommittee on 21st Century Competitiveness. The subcommittee took no action on the bill.

The Safe at Work Act

On November 1, 2005, Representative Rosa DeLauro (D-CN) introduced the Safe at Work Act (H.R. 4190). The bill was referred to the House Committee on Education and the Workforce and, on March 24, 2006, to the Subcommittee on Workforce Protections. No action was taken on the proposal.

The DeLauro bill was divided into two parts: First, the bill required that the Secretary of Labor "not enter into any agreement to provide any person with notice prior to commencing an investigation or inspection." Second, it required the Comptroller General to conduct a study of violations of child labor laws "including the number and type of allegations of child labor violations, when and whether inspections or investigations commenced for each such allegation, what enforcement action or other outcome resulted from such inspections or investigations, and a comparison of the extent to which such violations occurred in both large and small businesses.... " The time period for the Comptroller General's study was five years prior to the date of enactment.

The 108th Congress

The Traveling Sales Crew Protection Act

On September 23, 2003, Representative Tom Lantos (D-CA) introduced H.R. 3139, the Youth Worker Protection Act, one component of which was the provision that "No employer may employ a minor [a person under 18 years of age] in youth peddling." The bill, which went on to define what is included within the concept of "peddling," was referred to the Committee on Education and the Workforce and, in mid-October 2003, to the Subcommittee on Workforce Protections.

Some Questions of Public Policy

Periodically through recent years, concerns have been raised about the welfare of young persons (the age varies) who are engaged in certain types of outside sales work. On occasion, the focus has been upon the "street trades": selling newspapers, candy, or other items at subway stops or, locally, from door-to-door. In such cases, a manager or supervisor may recruit young persons, move them to various local sites and, at day's end, collect them and bring them back to their homes. But, there is also another arrangement: the "traveling sales crews" in which a sales team goes on the road and remains away from its home base, possibly for extended periods. Some argue that each of these types of sales ("peddling") can encompass risks, especially for young persons.

Such sales work by young persons suggests numerous questions of public policy. For example, how young is too young for children to be engaged in street sales, potentially in rough neighborhoods with which they may not be familiar? And, if they do engage in such work, through what hours should they be employed: how early in the morning and how late at night?

The situation becomes more complicated when groups of recruits are transported from their homes to a distant city to engage in sales work. Are the vehicles in which they are transported safe and insured? How and where are these workers housed? Does the manager or supervisor have authority and responsibility with respect to the off-hours behavior of these young workers? What happens if one of these young persons becomes ill and needs medical attention?

Beyond the personal, there are strictly workplace questions. What is the employment relationship between these workers and the manager or supervisor? Are the youth workers employees, independent contractors, or something else entirely? To the extent that they are employees, by whom are they employed? The manager or supervisor may also be an employee of some more distant entity. Where does responsibility ultimately reside? How are wages and benefits handled? What employment records are maintained—and by whom?

From a policy perspective, some may ask: Should young persons be excluded, by law, from working in street or door-to-door sales or in related support services other than actual selling? Were otherwise applicable hours restrictions to be observed, would such work be acceptable? Would a blanket prohibition on outside sales work by persons under 18 years of age unduly restrict their capacity to earn? Is there something inherently inappropriate about street sales or door-to-door sales? Is such work wrong when 16- and 17-year-olds are involved, but a legitimate entrepreneurial activity if all of the sales staff (and, perhaps, support staff) are 18 and over? Is such work acceptable when confined to a certain radius from the permanent residence of the sales staff? And, how expansive should that radius be?

The Wyden Initiative

In May 1985 (the 99th Congress), then-Representative Ron Wyden (D-OR), stating that "unscrupulous door-to-door selling groups" were exploiting young persons (some of them, children; others, young adults), introduced legislation to establish a National Clearinghouse on Fraudulent Youth Employment Practices. While Wyden conceded that "the vast majority of door-to-door sellers are wholly honorable and reputable," others, he suggested, were not. These companies "can be peddling anything from magazine subscriptions to chemical cleaners." He outlined a host of alleged violations of law and fraudulent sales practices engaged in by such firms and urged his colleagues to help "put these dangerous and unscrupulous operators out of business. And ... take a step toward protecting our youth from dangerous employment practices."[69]

Hearings were conducted (November 1985) by the House Subcommittee on Civil and Constitutional Rights. Susan Meisinger, speaking for the Reagan Labor Department, testified that there was indeed a problem. "Unlawful practices reported by the States include violations of their

---

[69] *Congressional Record*, May 16, 1985, p. E2251.

child labor laws, violations of minimum wage laws, employer failure to pay taxes and unemployment insurance, and abuse of child workers," Meisinger noted, "including forcing them to pay kickbacks, child molesting, and placing them in high risk, late night employment environments."[70]

But the Reagan Administration was divided on the issue. Victoria Toensing, representing the Department of Justice, agreed that "problems relating to the recruitment and use of salespersons do exist" but she suggested that any legislative action would be premature. "The extent of these problems has not yet been established," Toensing stated, and, in any case, state and local authorities "may be as effective, if not more so, than the federal government in preventing such abuses." Further, she suggested, not all of the alleged worker/victims were minors. After reviewing a series of federal statutes that might apply if there actually were a problem, Toensing noted that the Department of Justice "... considers present statutory provisions adequate."[71]

The Wyden bill (H.R. 2544) died at the close of the 99th Congress. Hearings on the general issue were subsequently conducted by the Senate Permanent Subcommittee on Investigations (1987)[72] and by the House Committee on Government Operations' Subcommittee on Employment and Housing (1990).[73] In each case, the matter was restricted to general oversight. Further legislation was not then proposed.[74]

The Kohl Proposals

In November 1999 (the 106th Congress), Senator Kohl introduced S. 1989, the Traveling Sales Crew Protection Act—his interest sparked by an auto accident in Wisconsin in which seven young people were killed and others injured. The Senator explained: "The driver [in the Wisconsin case] had a suspended license and a series of violations." These firms, he stated, "employ crews who travel from city to city selling products door to door. Often times," he asserted, "... [they] mistreat their workers and violate local, state, and federal labor law. Because they rapidly move from state to state, enforcement efforts are difficult if not impossible for local authorities." Senator Kohl recalled that it had been 12 years since the hearing by the Permanent Subcommittee on Investigations (noted above) and affirmed: "... nothing has changed. These abuses continue, and Congress should act."[75] But, no action was taken: the bill died at the close of the 106th Congress.

Early in the 107th Congress, Senator Kohl introduced new traveling sales crew/peddling legislation (S. 96). The Kohl bill would have amended the FLSA to provide that "No individual

---

[70] Statement of Susan R. Meisinger, Deputy Under Secretary for Employment Standards, DOL, November 6, 1985, the House Judiciary Subcommittee on Civil and Constitutional Rights.

[71] Statement of Victoria Toensing, Deputy Assistant Attorney General, Criminal Division, November 6, 1985, the House Judiciary Subcommittee on Civil and Constitutional Rights.

[72] U.S. Congress, Senate Committee on Governmental Affairs. Permanent Subcommittee on Investigations, *Exploitation of Young Adults in Door-to-Door Sales*, hearing, 100th Cong., 1st sess., April 6, 1987, 217 p.

[73] U.S. Congress, House Committee on Government Operations, Subcommittee on Employment and Housing, *Children at Risk in the Workplace*, hearing, 101st Cong., 2nd sess., March 16, June 8, 1990, pp. 277-297.

[74] The issue, however defined, continued to arise periodically. See Jim Naughton, "Children's Candy Sales Are Criticized: Distributors Under Scrutiny for Possible Child Labor Infractions," *The Washington Post*, May 9, 1990, pp. A1, A10; "State Trying To Close Down Firm Employing Youngsters," *The Daily Olympian*, October 15, 1990, pp. C1-C2; and Julie Barrett, "Kiddie Hawkers," *Generation Next*, July/August 1995, pp. 22-23.

[75] *Congressional Record*, November 19, 1999, p. S15102.

under 18 years of age may be employed in a position requiring the individual to engage in door to door sales or in related support work in a manner that requires the individual to remain away from his or her permanent residence for more than 24 hours." After defining the operative language, the bill set forth a registration requirement for employers and supervisors of traveling sales crew workers. Then, assuming that such practices were to be allowed, it outlined the obligations of the parties—dealing with such issues as housing, transportation, wages (and deductions therefrom), insurance, and related matters. It then proposed a system for enforcement.

A comprehensive and detailed proposal, S. 96 was referred to the Committee on Health, Education, Labor and Pensions (HELP) where no action was taken.[76] Then, on May 22, 2002, Senator Kohl introduced S. 2549, an abbreviated version of the traveling sales crew/peddling legislation. An amendment to Section 12 of the FLSA, S. 2549 read, in pertinent part:

> No individual under 18 years of age may be employed in a position requiring the individual to engage in door to door sales or in related support work in a manner that requires the individual to remain away from his or her permanent residence for more than 24 hours.

It further authorized the Secretary of Labor to "issue such rules and regulations as are necessary to carry out" the proposed amendment. On August 1, 2002, the HELP Committee, to which the bill had been referred, was discharged from further consideration and the bill, under unanimous consent, was agreed to by the Senate.[77] It was referred to the House Committee on Education and the Workforce, Subcommittee on Workforce Protections, where it died at the close of the 107th Congress.

The issue was raised in the 108th Congress, again in an abbreviated form, with introduction of H.R. 3139 by Representative Lantos: an umbrella child labor reform proposal, discussed below. No action, however, was taken on the Lantos bill.[78] In the 109th Congress, Lantos again introduced the issue as part of H.R. 2870, a general bill dealing with child labor. But once more, the bill was directed to the Subcommittee on Workforce Protections, where it remained.

Sawmilling/Woodworking by 14-Year-Olds

On May 1, 2003, legislation to permit employment of young persons (of at least 14 years of age) in sawmilling and woodworking facilities was introduced by Representative Joseph Pitts (R-PA) and Senator Arlen Specter (R-PA)—respectively H.R. 1943 and S. 974. On October 8, 2003, a hearing on the Pitts bill was conducted by the House Subcommittee on Workforce Protections.

A Question of Public Policy

Work in or around sawmills and wood-working machinery has been deemed by DOL as especially hazardous for persons under 18 years of age. The practice violates at least two

---

[76] A somewhat condensed version of the legislation (H.R. 3070) was introduced in the House during the 107th Congress by Representative Thomas Petri (R-WI). No action was taken on the Petri bill.

[77] *Congressional Record*, August 1, 2002, p. S8022.

[78] *Congressional Record*, September 24, 2003, pp. E1873-E1874.

Departmental Hazardous Occupations (HO) Orders: HO 4, covering sawmills, and HO 5, dealing with power-driven woodworking machines.[79]

Speaking generally, the Amish resist requirements of law that would alter their traditional way of life and have rejected compulsory school attendance beyond the 8th grade. The *Daily Labor Report* explains: "After completing their formal classroom training [elementary school] at age 14 or 15, Amish boys typically receive training in farming or carpentry from their fathers."[80] In recent years, the opportunity for the Amish to farm has diminished—in part, because of increased land values and property taxes. Therefore, the Amish have sought other activities for their children. "What are we supposed to do with them if they don't work here," lamented one member of the Amish community, "have them stay on the street all day?"[81]

The Amish have sought to have their sons work in sawmills and woodworking plants where there is Amish supervision (or where they are supervised by an adult relative).[82] The Department of Labor has held that permitting children to work in such plants would be a violation of federal child labor law: HO 4 and HO 5. The result has been a clash between the Amish and DOL. The Amish have pressed for an amendment to the child labor provisions of the FLSA in order to accommodate their practices.

Taking the Issue to Congress

At least since the 105th Congress, legislation to amend federal child labor law on behalf of the Amish has been repeatedly introduced, both in the House and in the Senate. The bills, generally, would widen the opportunity for youth ages 14 to 18 "to be employed inside or outside places of business where machinery is used to process wood products." In order to qualify for such employment, a youth would have to be "a member of a religious sect or division thereof whose established teachings do not permit formal education beyond the eighth grade." In the 105th and 106th Congresses, the Amish legislation was passed by the House under suspension but the Senate did not act.[83]

---

[79] See 29 C.F.R. §§570.54 and 750.55. In a letter of July 22, 1998, to Chairman William F. Goodling (R-PA), then-Chair of the Committee on Education and the Workforce, Deputy Secretary of Labor Kathryn Higgins explained the special hazards associated with work in the lumber and wood products industry which, she said, were "exacerbated for youth" given their "lack of training" and "immaturity."

[80] Bureau of National Affairs, *Daily Labor Report*, July 23, 1998, p. A11. Concerning the Amish perspective on public education, see Gertrude Enders Huntington, "Persistence and Change in Amish Education," in Donald B. Kraybill and Marc A. Olshan (eds.), *The Amish Struggle with Modernity* (Hanover, New Hampshire: University Press of New England, 1994), pp.77-95; and Thomas J. Meyers, "Education and Schooling," in Kraybill (ed.), *The Amish and the State* (Baltimore: The Johns Hopkins University Press, 2003), pp. 87-106.

[81] Steven Greenhouse, "Foes of Idle Hands, Amish Contest a Child Labor Law," *The New York Times*, October 18, 2003, p. A1.

[82] Ibid. The issue involves sons, not daughters. Greenhouse explains, p. 9, "Teenage girls, as always, learn skills like quilting or work in retail shops." See also Marc A. Olshan and Kimberly D. Schmidt, "Amish Women and the Feminist Conundrum," in Kraybill and Olshan (eds.), pp. 215-230.

[83] *Congressional Record*, September 28, 1998, pp. H9121-H9124. See also U.S. Congress, House Committee on Education and the Workforce, Subcommittee on Workforce Protections, *The Effect of the Fair Labor Standards Act on Amish Families and H.R. 2038, the MSPA Clarification Act*, hearing, 105th Cong., 2nd sess., April 21, 1998 (Washington: GPO, 1998); and U.S. Congress, House Committee on Education and the Workforce, *Amending the Fair Labor Standards Act of 1938 To Permit Certain Youth To Perform Certain Work with Wood Products*, report together with minority views to accompany H.R. 221, H.Rept. 106-31, 106th Cong., 1st sess., (Washington: GPO, 1999), 29 p.

Had the legislation been adopted, Amish children, having left school after the 8th grade, could have been employed in work otherwise regarded as too hazardous for persons under 18 years of age. Some have suggested that constitutional issues may be involved in affording special treatment to the Amish that is not afforded to other religious groups. Setting aside issues of legality, other questions could be raised, given that Amish children are permitted to leave school after the 8th grade.[84] First, would elimination of federal restrictions upon child labor—to the extent proposed in the legislation—provide an opportunity (and, perhaps, an incentive) for Amish children to leave school and to enter the world-of-work? Or, would it merely recognize that Amish children are already out of school and, thus, permit them to be productively occupied? Second, assuming that these children do leave school to work, are sawmills and wood processing establishments appropriate places of employment for any youngsters under the age of 18? Might other areas of skills training be more suitable for children than mill work with its attendant hazards? What types of work are suitable for 14-year-old Amish children and who should decide?[85]

In order to strengthen the ties of Amish children to the Amish community, youngsters are systematically separated from the non-Amish world.[86] The work experience of Amish children with the skills they acquire on the family farm may not be readily transferable to the non-Amish marketplace. Thus, with only an 8th-grade education and lacking experience in the non-Amish world, their subsequent choices may be, accordingly, restricted, rendering their out-migration from the community within which they were raised extremely difficult.[87] Some may applaud this result; others may question the appropriateness of a federal role in its facilitation.

On May 3, 2001, the Senate Appropriations Subcommittee on Labor, Health and Human Services, and Education, conducted an oversight hearing on the employment needs of Amish youth. Representative Mark Souder (R-IN) spoke in support of exemption. Mr. Souder, representing a partly Amish constituency, explained that the Amish had not been able to persuade DOL to acquiesce in industrial employment for Amish children at age 14. Urging amendment of the FLSA to permit such employment, he argued that the Amish children would be "supervised by adults who know and care about them" and that the proposed amendment "would protect a truly endangered religion and culture."[88]

Thomas M. Markey of DOL testified in opposition, arguing: "Sawmills are dangerous places to work, even for adults." Pointing to a high accident and fatality rate for the industry nationwide, he stated that such work is "even more dangerous for children."[89]

---

[84] The issue of school attendance is developed in some detail in *Wisconsin v. Yoder*, 406 U.S. 205 (1972).

[85] The proposed legislation deals narrowly with employment of children in sawmills and related woodworking establishments. Their employment in other fields, currently restricted by law or by administrative ruling, would require separate action.

[86] Jennifer Brown, "Old Ways Persevere, Flourish: Non-Mainstream Culture Helps Anabaptist Communities Retain Hold on the Young," *The Washington Post*, April 21, 2001, p. B9.

[87] These issues are discussed in Joel Feinberg, "The Child's Right to an Open Future," in William Aiken and Hugh LaFollette (eds.), *Whose Child? Children's Rights, Parental Authority, and State Power* (Totowa, N.J.: Rowman and Littlefield, 1980), pp. 124-153; and Dena S. Davis, "The Child's Right to an Open Future: *Yoder* and Beyond," *Capital University Law Review*, vol. 26 (1997), pp. 93-105. See also Albert N. Keim (ed.), *Compulsory Education and the Amish: The Right Not to Be Modern* (Boston: Beacon Press, 1975).

[88] Testimony of Representative Mark Souder before the Senate Subcommittee on Labor, Health and Human Services and Education, Committee on Appropriations, May 3, 2001.

[89] Testimony of Thomas M. Markey, Acting Administrator, Wage and Hour Division, U.S. Department of Labor, (continued...)

On June 13, 2001, during consideration of S. 1 (reauthorization of the Elementary and Secondary Education Act), Senator Specter proposed S.Amdt. 420. It would have amended the FLSA to permit Amish youngsters, 14 years of age and older, to work, under specified conditions, in mills and woodworking plants. Senator Edward M. Kennedy (D-MA), chairman of the Committee on Health, Education, Labor, and Pensions (HELP), and Senator Specter engaged in a brief debate. Senator Kennedy affirmed that it "would be valuable to have ... an open hearing" on the issue—particularly with respect to the safety of prospective workers—and agreed that his committee would conduct such a hearing. With that understanding, Senator Specter then withdrew his proposed amendment.[90]

On July 25, 2001, legislation to permit Amish youth to work at age 14 in wood processing plants was introduced both in the House and in the Senate: H.R. 2639 (Pitts) and S. 1241 (Specter). No action was taken on these proposals.

Revived in the 108th Congress

The Pitts (H.R. 1943) and Specter (S. 974) bills of the 108th Congress largely follow the pattern of recent years. To be exempt from the restraints of federal child labor law, several standards would be imposed.

The targeted youth must be "at least 14" years of age. Further, the child:

> (a) Must be "by statute or judicial order ... exempt from compulsory school attendance beyond the eighth grade."[91]

> (b) Must be "supervised by an adult relative" or "by an adult member of the same religious sect or division as the individual."

> (c) May not "operate or assist in the operation of power-driven woodworking machines."

> (d) Must be "protected from wood particles or other flying debris within the workplace by a barrier appropriate to the potential hazard of such wood particles or flying debris or by maintaining a sufficient distance from machinery in operation ... "

> (e) "[I]is required to use personal protective equipment to prevent exposure to excessive levels of noise and saw dust."

Other concerns aside, some may ask: Would the safeguards be adequate? In the absence of frequent DOL inspections, would the precautions be observed? Does the fact that a supervisor would be of "the same religious sect" as the child worker render the work any less hazardous—or the supervisor any more diligent in monitoring the youth's work?

(...continued)

before the Subcommittee on Labor, Health and Human Services, and Education, Committee on Appropriations, U.S. Senate, May 3, 2001.

[90] *Congressional Record*, June 13, 2001, pp. S6153-S6154.

[91] The wording is from S. 974. The phrasing of H.R. 1943 is slightly different.

On October 8, 2003, the Subcommittee on Workforce Protections conducted a hearing on H.R. 1943. In an opening statement, Chairman Charlie Norwood (R-GA) observed that the bill provides:

> that certain youth whose religious faith and beliefs dictate that they "learn by doing" are afforded an opportunity to do so, and that the federal government—however well-meaning— does not endanger the belief and culture of these young people and their families.[92]

As the lead witness (DOL was not represented at the hearing), Representative Pitts stated that actions of the department had "severely threatened the lifestyle and religion of this respected and humble community" and averred that the "government should not interfere" with Amish practices lest "their strong heritage ... be undermined."[93] Representative Mark Souder (R-IN), while reviewing the proposed safeguards embodied in the amendment, also framed the issue in religious terms. Government bureaucracy, he stated, "... is threatening the Amish people's very way of life. It is interfering with their religious freedom."[94] Christ K. Blank, speaking for the Old Order Amish, concurred, declaring "the ages 14 through 17 to be a very tender receptive age" and a period during which "to instill ... Amish values and work ethics in our children."[95]

But, not all were in complete agreement. Nicholas Clark of the United Food and Commercial Workers, AFL-CIO, recognized the religious desires of the Amish community. He pointed out, however, that federal government studies had found that working conditions in "sawmilling and woodworking are among the most hazardous occupations for adults, with a death rate that is *five times* the national average for all industries," and that such work is "especially inappropriate for young workers" (emphasis in the original). Clark expressed concern about constitutional issues and raised, as well, the issue of equity. The proposed amendment "... would grant Amish-owned sawmills and woodworking firms an exception from child labor laws that are [sic] denied firms owned by persons of non-Amish faiths." Further, he argued, it would deny "Amish children the very real benefits of governmental health and safety protections that are afforded Catholic, Baptist, Jewish or any other" non-Amish children. While sawmills and woodworking plants "provide much needed employment for Amish adults," he concluded, "they cannot safely or constitutionally serve that purpose for Amish children."[96]

Amish Child Workers and the 2004 Appropriations Bill

As the first session of the 108th Congress moved to a close, several appropriations bills (among them, the measure providing funding for the Department of Labor) remained to be passed. Ultimately, the several appropriations bills were combined in H.R. 2673, the FY2004 Consolidated Appropriations bill.

---

[92] Opening statement of Chairman Norwood, October 8, 2003.

[93] Testimony of Representative Pitts, October 8, 2003.

[94] Testimony of Representative Souder, October 8, 2003.

[95] Testimony of Christ K. Blank, Chairman, Voice of the Old Order Amish, Old Order Amish Steering Committee, October 8, 2003.

[96] Testimony of Nicholas Clark, October 8, 2003. Clark stated: "The proposal would also require government investigators to determine whether owners of firms seeking to employ child labor, and their child employees, are truly Amish. Such determinations would necessarily entangle the government in the practice of religion, also in violation of the First Amendment."

A conference report on H.R. 2673 (H.Rept. 108-401) was filed on November 25, 2003. Included in the conference report (Senator Specter had served as a Senate conferee) was language roughly paralleling that of H.R. 1943, the Amish child labor bill. In an explanation of the measure, the conference report stated:

> The conference agreement includes a provision to permit youth, ages 14 through 17, who by statute or judicial order are exempt from compulsory school attendance beyond the eighth grade, to work inside or outside places of business where machinery is used to process wood products. The youth would be permitted to perform activities such as sweeping, stacking wood, and writing orders. Safety provisions include prohibiting the youth from operating machinery, and requiring the use of eye and body protections.

On December 8, 2003, the House voted to approve the conference report (with the Amish child labor provision included). The vote was 242 yeas to 176 nays.[97] Senate consideration of the measure was deferred until the second session of the 108th Congress.[98] On January 20 and 22, the Senate considered the conference report, though attention appears to have focused on overtime pay regulations and subjects other than the Amish child labor provision. On January 22, the Senate approved the conference report by a vote of 65 yeas to 28 nays.[99] The measure was signed by the President on January 23, 2004 (P.L. 108-199).

In a statement to the press, Senator Specter noted that he had "toured an Amish sawmill in Lancaster County, PA," had met with some members of the Amish people, and had come to "know of the importance of this legislation to their community and culture. This is an issue of freedom of religion," he affirmed, "where the Amish prefer to educate their children aside from the public schools and part of that educational process is for teenagers to work in the lumber mills."[100]

Author Contact Information

Gerald Mayer
Analyst in Labor Policy
gmayer@crs.loc.gov, 7-7815

Acknowledgments

This report is an update of a CRS report originally written by William G. Whittaker.

---

[97] *Congressional Record*, December 8, 2003, p. 12845.

[98] U.S. Congress, Conference Committees, *Making Appropriations for Agriculture, Rural Development, Food and Drug Administration, and Related Agencies for the Fiscal Year Ending September 30, 2004, and for Other Purposes*, conference report to accompany H.R. 2673, 108th Cong., 1st sess., H.Rept. 108-401 (Washington, GPO, 2003), pp. 734 and 235-236. See also *DLR* December 3, 2003, pp. A11-A12.

[99] *Congressional Record*, January 22, 2004, pp. S155-S156.

[100] Press release, Office of Senator Arlen Specter, January 23, 2004, the Senator's website, visited on January 29, 2004.